# START-UP
# SCIENCE

# MATERIALS

## Claire Llewellyn

Evans

Published by Evans Brothers Limited
2A Portman Mansions
Chiltern Street
London W1U 6NR

© Evans Brothers Limited 2004

Produced for Evans Brothers Limited by
White-Thomson Publishing Ltd.
2/3 St Andrew's Place
Lewes, East Sussex BN7 1UP

Printed in China by WKT Company Limited

Editor: Dereen Taylor
Consultants: Les Jones, Science Consultant, Manchester
Education Partnership, Norah Granger, former primary
headteacher and senior lecturer in education, University
of Brighton
Designer: Leishman Design

Cover: All photographs by Chris Fairclough.

British Library Cataloguing in Publication Data
Llewellyn, Claire
    Materials - (Start-up science)
    1.Materials - Juvenile literature
    I.Title
    620.1'1

ISBN: 0 237 52590 9

Acknowledgements:
Special thanks to the following for their help and
involvement in the preparation of this book: Staff and
pupils at Elm Grove Primary School, Brighton, Liz
Price and family and friends, Christine Clark and family.

Picture Acknowledgements:
Chris Fairclough Colour Library 21;
Corbis 17 (top left), 18.
All other photographs by Chris Fairclough.

# Contents

# All kinds of materials

Tom and Olivia are having a picnic.

They are putting everything they need on a picnic table.

These objects are made of different materials.

objects materials feel hard shiny

Each material has its own look and feel. Which ones are hard? Which ones are shiny?

plastic cup

wooden pepper pot

glass jug

metal knife and fork

paper napkins

plastic   wooden   glass   metal   paper   5

# Choosing materials

▶ Phoebe is one year old. Her parents choose her things with care. They think about what materials they are made of.

The plastic tray on this high chair is strong and easy to clean.

Why do you think they chose a board book for Phoebe?

Why do you think they chose a woolly teddy?

strong  easy  clean  board

When Phoebe eats, she wears a bib to protect her clothes from food. What kind of material makes a good bib?

▶ Ali is testing three different materials: paper, towelling and plastic.

He puts each material on top of a white cloth, then he pours juice on each one in turn.

Which one do you think makes the best bib?

woolly    protect    testing

# Natural materials

Justin is a carpenter. He works with **wood**. Wood comes from trees. It is a **natural** material. Natural materials are found in the **world** around us.

▶ Justin **cuts** the **planks** of wood on a saw.

wood   natural   world

◄ What did Justin have to do to the wood to make this door frame?

▼ Wood can also be used to make paper. You see tiny bits of wood in some kinds of paper.

cuts   planks

# Building with natural materials

▶ **This house is made of bricks, stone and wood.**

**The bricks are made from clay, which is dug out of the ground.**

**Do you know where the stone comes from?**

Bricks ...........➤

Stone ..........➤

Wood ..........➤


bricks   stone   clay

Builders **choose materials that are strong and hard-wearing.**

▲ **Olivia wants to build a bridge over her railway track.**

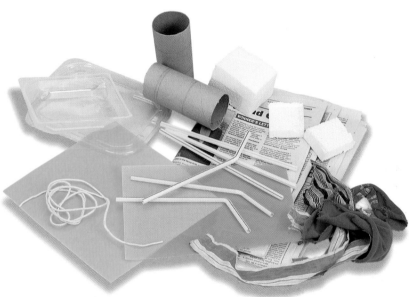

▲ **Which of these materials would you choose to make a bridge?**

**How would you make it?**

# Making materials

Some materials are not natural. They are manufactured.

Plastic is not a natural material. It was invented by scientists, who made it out of oil.

There are hundreds of kinds of plastic. Each one looks and feels different, and is used for different things.

► These sunglasses use two different kinds of plastic.

CE © Gullane (Thomas) Limited 2003

hard and colourful plastic

see-through plastic

manufactured   scientists

strong    hard    soft

stretchy

waterproof

washable

light

colourful    bendy    spongy

**Which of these words would you use to describe the plastic objects in the pictures? Can you think of any other things that are made of plastic?**

oil    describe

# Magnetic materials

**Magnets have an invisible force that pulls things towards them.**

▼ **Ernest tests his magnet on things made of different materials.**

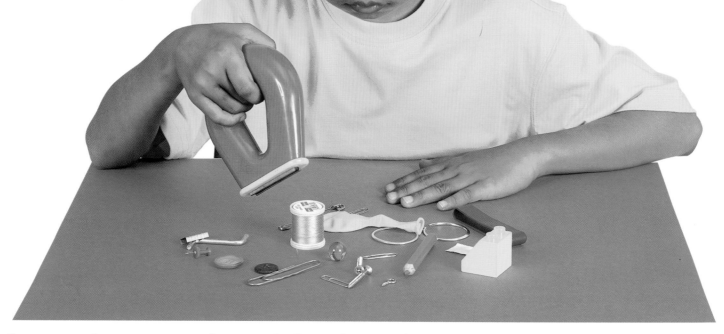

**Objects that can be picked up by a magnet are magnetic Magnetic objects are always made of metal.**

magnets   force   magnetic

▲ See how many metal objects you can pick up with a magnet.

Not everything made of metal is magnetic.

► Look at the cans in the picture. What does the magnet tell us about them?

# Changing shape

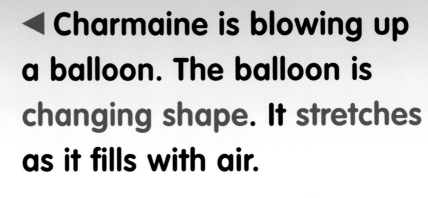

◄ Charmaine is blowing up a balloon. The balloon is changing shape. It stretches as it fills with air.

What will happen when Charmaine lets the air out?

Some materials hold a new shape. Others spring back when you let them go.

changing  shape  stretches

◄ **Keith is making a mug out of clay.**

He **squashes** and **bends** the clay until it is the right shape.

► **We can change the shape of many materials. What could you do to these objects to change their shape?**

hold  spring back  squashes  bends  **17**

# Heat changes things

▶ Keith's clay mug is not very strong. He puts it into an **oven** called a kiln. The oven's **heat hardens** the clay and makes the mug **stronger**.

Heat can change some materials. Changes like this often last for ever. You cannot change them back.

**Cooking** is a way of changing some foods, making them **safer** to eat.

**⚡WARNING!**
Ovens are dangerous.
Never cook by yourself.

oven   heat   hardens

▶ Make a chart to compare each of these foods before and after cooking.

| Food | Before cooking | After cooking |
| --- | --- | --- |
| Pasta | hard, brittle, not good to eat | Soft, squidgy, good to eat |
| Eggs | | |
| Sausages | | |

stronger    cooking    safer    soft

# Cooling materials

▶ Rosie is making ice lollies. She pours fruit juice into the moulds. Then she puts them in the freezer.

◀ Three hours later, she takes one out. How has the fruit juice changed? What other things change when you put them in the freezer?


ice   pours   moulds   freezer

Many materials change as they cool. Look at the two pictures.

◄ What does the jelly look like when it is hot?

► What does it look like when it is cold?

cool   hot   cold

21

# Further information for

## Possible Activities

### PAGES 4–5

Make a collection of objects made from many different materials. Label them.

Ask children to identify objects (e.g. wooden beads, metal key, soap) with their eyes closed. How do they manage to do this?

### PAGES 6–7

Make a puppet using different materials. Draw a picture of the puppet, labelling the materials and explaining why they were chosen (e.g. "I used wool for the hair because it is long and stringy.")

Ask the children to make a greetings card. Think what kind of paper/card will be most suitable for the job. Why? Test out their ideas.

### PAGES 8–9

Make a display of wooden materials. Use reference books or CDs to find out more about the uses of wood.

### PAGES 10–11

Collect pictures of natural materials and the products they are used to make (e.g. sheep's wool/a woollen scarf; reeds/thatched roof). Can children match the material to the product?

Ask children to make a toy slide. What kind of materials would be suitable and why? Get them to test their ideas.

### PAGES 12–13

Make a collection of plastic objects. Group and label them according to their characteristics.

Make a collection of items made of paper, such as tissue paper, cardboard, kitchen roll, etc. What words describe the different kinds of paper? Now sort the items into different groups.

### PAGES 14–15

Make a collection of different kinds of magnet.

Make a magnetic fishing game with fish cut out of foil and a fishing rod made of a stick, some string and a magnet.

# Parents and Teachers

Slide paper clips onto the fish and drop them in a bowl of water. How many can you catch?

## PAGES 16–17

Ask children to collect a number of objects (e.g. a towel, a banana, a stone) and test whether they will stretch, bend, squash or twist. Compile the results on a chart.

Explore the properties of elastic bands, foam sponges and soft rubber balls. What happens when you squash and stretch these?

## PAGES 18–19

Give children the ingredients for scones to mix. Bake them and look at the finished scones together. Can the children describe the differences they observe before and after heating?

Why do we boil eggs? Show children a raw and a hard-boiled egg. Discuss the differences between them.

Discuss which foods we eat raw and which we eat cooked. Why do we cook some foods and not others?

## PAGES 20–21

Make some ice cubes in the freezer. Now leave them out around the classroom. How long do they take to melt? Which ones melt first and why?

Make some crispy cakes by stirring cornflakes into some melted chocolate and spooning the mixture into paper cases. What happens as they cool?

Glass hardens as it cools. Use a reference book to find out how glass objects are made.

## Further Information

### BOOKS FOR CHILDREN

*All Kinds of Everything* by Sam Godwin
(Hodder Wayland, 2002)

*Find Out About* series by Henry Pluckrose
(Franklin Watts, 2002)

*Science Starters: Super Materials* by Wendy Madgwick
(Hodder Wayland, 2002)

*Ways Into Science: Changing Materials/Materials* by Peter Riley
(Franklin Watts, 2001)

*Why Can't I Sleep on a Bed of Bubbles? and Other Questions about Materials* by Sally Hewitt
(Belitha Press, 2001)

### BOOKS FOR ADULTS

*How to Sparkle at Science Investigations* by Monica Huns
(Brilliant Publications)

### WEBSITES

www.howstuffworks.com
www.primaryresources.co.uk/science